GW00360326

The Lord is My Shepherd

from Psalm 23

Ingrid Beck

Psalm 23
A Psalm of David

The Lord is my Shepherd;

I have everything I need.

He makes me lie down in green pastures;

He leads me beside quiet waters.

He restores my soul;

He leads me on paths that are right for

his name's sake.

Even though I walk through the valley of the shadow of death,
I will fear no evil; for you are with me.
Your rod and your staff, they comfort me.

You prepare a table before me in the presence of my enemies.
You anoint my head with oil;
My cup overflows.
Surely goodness and mercy will follow me all the days of my life;
and I will dwell in the house of the Lord forever.

The Lord looks after me.

*H*e makes sure I have everything I need.

*H*e gives me green grass to lie down in,

And quiet waters to enjoy.

*H*e makes me feel so good,

*A*nd he tells me the right things to do.

*E*ven though I may be in frightening situations, I never need to be scared, for I know the Lord is always with me, although I cannot see him.

Our Father
who is in Heaven.
Hallowed be your name
Your kingdom come,
your Will be done,
on Earth, as it is
in Heaven.

He comforts me,

Give us today our daily bread, and forgive us our sins, as we forgive those who sin against us. Lead us not into temptation, but deliver us from evil, for the kingdom, the power, and the glory are yours forever and ever. Amen.

and looks after me.

The Lord makes sure I have food to eat, and he keeps my enemies away from me.

*H*e blesses me.

And because he is so good,
I feel so happy inside.

I am sure goodness and love will
follow me all of my life.

And one day I shall go to live in
the Lord's house, forever.

ISBN 1-85608-400-0

Designed by Graham Whiteman

Write to: Hunt & Thorpe, Deershot Lodge, Park Lane, Ropley, Alresford, Hampshire SO24 0BE, UK

Hunt & Thorpe is a name used under licence by Paternoster Publishing,
PO Box 300, Kingstown Broadway, Carlisle, CA3 0QS

A CIP catalague record for this book is available from the British Library

Printed in Hong Kong/China

paternoster
publishing

HUNT&
THORPE